UNDERNOSE
FARM

FOR RITA

AUTHOR ROYALTIES ARE BEING
DONATED TO THE
PETER MCVERRY TRUST.

UNDERNOSE FARM

Harry Crosbie

THE LILLIPUT PRESS
DUBLIN

First published 2020 by

THE LILLIPUT PRESS LTD
62–63 Sitric Road, Arbour Hill, Dublin 7, Ireland
www.lilliputpress.ie

ISBN 978 18435 18099

A CIP record is available from the British Library.

3 5 7 9 10 8 6 4 2

Set in 12pt on 17pt Scala by Niall McCormack
Printed in Kerry and bound in Dublin

CONTENTS

1
EIGHTEEN AND A HALF

Adventure. You want adventure? I'll give you adventure.

I was eighteen and a half, my mother told me I was gorgeous. Long black hair down my back, stiff-legged walk like Gene Pitney on the telly. Could not care less: cool – no, I mean *totally* cool; cool as the Lone Ranger.

It was 1965, I had left school, burnt the books, it was a long summer. I was ready, man!

I had been in a skiffle group with Fran O'Toole from Bray. I was a Bengal – chancer to you – but he was a naturally gifted musician, bastard. I went to see him in my uncle's Morris Minor van. His father owned a bingo hall. At that time, English mill workers still came to Bray for their holidays. Mad or what?

Girls, girls, girls everywhere. One quiet afternoon the manager was sick (i.e. drunk) and I got to call out the bingo. Totally cool.

I did it real slow. Smouldering. My bird was up the front: cheeky, cowboy hat, fringes, factory girl – classy. Boy heaven. See you later, alligator, I said with my eyes.

There was a phone outside Fran's house. Press Button B, sickly green. I had promised to call a new friend, a hippy head from Bray, otherwise known as The Bray Head. Fur coat, beads, no socks: cool.

'Hey, man,' he said.

'Hey,' I said.

'Have you got £65?' he asked.

'No bother,' I said.

I had £12, my communion money. My granny was minding it, but my sisters were loaded and an easy touch.

'I'm gonna hitch to the Middle East,' he said.

'Cool,' I said, 'Good weed there, man.'

'Wanna come?' he asked.

'Does Dolly Parton sleep on her back?' Boys of eighteen should be chained to a radiator until their brains switch on.

'The mail boat is Friday, 7 pm,' The Head said.

'Bring it on.'

'We travel light,' he said. 'One rucksack only.'

'I don't have a rucksack.'

'Capel Street, Cheeky Charlie's,' he said.

I told my mother I was going to see a friend for a few days. She packed a little case for me with beautifully ironed pyjamas, hankies, socks, all tied in bows with green silk ribbons. She gave me a box of chocs for my friend's mother. Silk bows – what's that about?

It was a rough crossing. We drank eight pints with a crowd of Irish tinkers/horse dealers ... don't ask.

I threw the little case with its bows into an angry sea and gave the chocs to a couple of drunken girls. Cruel, cruel youth.

After a rain-sodden week of misery we got to a small German town. We stayed in the local dosshouse. 'Keep your hand on your halfpenny,' my granny told me.

We put the two end-legs of the bed into our boots and our money under the legs nearest the wall. There was a long row of beds, all with boots on. It was a funny, sad sight.

In the Munich beer halls we heard that Dachau was just outside the city. A group of us went next day. It really does say '*Arbeit Macht Frei*' on the gate. Then a strange and frightening thing happened. I could not go through the gate and into the camp – some sense of evil or force of remembered suffering stopped me like a blow in the chest. I waited outside for two hours. They laughed at me as they went in. There was no laughing coming out.

We were on the road to Istanbul, hippie head office for we alternative folk – property is theft. We hitched a big trailer truck heading for Syria. My war-comic German stood me in good stead. '*Wann ist der nächte Lastwagen, bitte?*' I asked. I told the Arab driver, my new friend, that my father was a capitalist and had trucks, and that I could drive heavy machinery.

Night fell, an empty moon hung over a desert road. He asked me to drive. The Bray Head was asleep in the bunk. The driver was impressed, up and down the gearbox, no bother. Dancing!

He rolled a spliff and then it happened: talking sweet and low, he put his hand on my leg (upper). I pushed it away and told him to stop. Nothing more for an hour. He was drinking whiskey, didn't offer me any. The mood darkened. Driving a big truck with blazing headlights on a moonlit desert road is a calm and beautiful thing. Eating up the miles, Arab music softly on the radio. Quiet. Then the hand again, upper upper, this time no sweet talk. I braked hard and pulled in with squealing tyres and a dust cloud. I cut the big diesel, sudden silence except the ticking of a cooling engine in the cold desert night air. I turned towards the bunk and shouted at The Bray Head to scarper.

We jumped down from the cab and rolled in between the trailer axles: I told you I was good with trucks. The driver stood out in the headlamp beams casting a long shadow into the desert. He had a heavy wrench in his hand and was looking for us. Not a happy camper. I put a finger to my lips to tell The Bray Head to keep shtum. It turned out he did not believe in fighting or war. Spare me – pacifism has its time and place. More likely he was a cowardy, cowardy custard.

I crawled along the chassis to the sow-belly box – again, don't ask – and got a steel pin. The driver had no night vision due to the blazing lamps. I ran out of the darkness and hit him hard. He went down like the proverbial. Lights out. 'Not tonight, Josephine,' I said. Good line under the circs, I thought.

I switched off the truck's lights and we walked all night, hiding from any traffic. We stayed for a week to 'rest up', as the cowboys say. Thessaloniki. Nice town, you should try it.

We stayed in the youth hostel. I met a beautiful blonde English girl. I know she fancied me as she completely ignored me and never looked at me. Girls and their little tricks, eh? One night we were all sitting out in the yard rolling our 'Soviet' spliff. Everyone puts in their gear, a forty-Rizla paper job, eighteen inches long. My new bird was kissing another bloke in front of me so I knew I was in. Oh, the games we play.

People don't give blood in Thessaloniki, they sell it. We sold our blood every day for five local dollars a litre. More money than God. I sent flip-flops to my mother. They would be handy for her around the house, I thought.

Then we heard there was a big dope dealer paying twenty dollars for European blood. Four Germans from our hostel said they would go and check it out. They did not turn up for our 'Soviet' that evening.

Early next morning I was in my *Schlafsack* (German again) up on the roof of the hostel. I woke to a heavy kick of a boot. Four policemen stood around me. Not a good start to one's day.

'Do you smoke dope?' one asked.

'Never,' I said.

'Have you got any dope now?' another asked.

'Definitely not,' I said. I gently moved my stash to the end of my *Schlafsack* with my foot.

'Do you know the four persons who left here last night?'

'Yes,' I said, 'they were Herman the German and his gang ... I mean group. We were expecting them home for our evening sing-song.'

'They are not coming back,' one said.

'Oh?' I said.

'Yes,' said another, 'they went to an illegal blood dealer. We found them lying on the beds still hooked up to the tubes. They had all the blood in their bodies drained completely.'

'Drained?' I said.

'Yes,' they said. 'Completely.'

'Are they all right?' I said.

'No, they are not all right, they are all dead. All four. Dead.'

My brain froze. I saw only my mother's beautifully ironed pyjamas with the little green bows.

I began to cry. I wanted to go home to her right then and beg her forgiveness. I wanted to fold her in my arms and touch her hair and tell her I had left as a stupid, stupid boy but now I was a man. I wanted to tell her I would do something every day of my life from now on to make her happy. I wanted to sit and eat buttery toast with her in the mornings. I wanted to tell her that now I understood her love and cherished it. I wanted to tell her I would bring her in our Morris Minor van to her favourite place in the world, a little seaside hotel in Wexford where she and my father got married. We would go for a paddle in the patient, gentle sea as we had always done on our summer holidays, before I grew up and became a man.

2
WALKING ON WATER

Mattie was a small man, a really small man, less than five feet tall. He had a big flat head and the local joke was that it would be a handy place to set down your pint when the pub was busy. Mattie was an inventor, artist, mechanic, designer, welder, carpenter, fitter, and he played the fiddle.

He walked on water: repeat, walked on water.

He was from a small village on the Shannon. He craved adventure as a young man and declared to the village that he would walk across the Shannon. He invented a pair of floating boots. These were five feet long, the same as himself. They were bright red with laces neatly tied and bowed. Long laces. Mattie explained that red was a navigational aid to ensure safety to other river traffic. Each boot had a rod standing up roughly where the big toe was located. This was connected to a flat board below, which led across the sole of the boot. When a step forward was taken the rod was pushed down so that the board dropped and bit into the water.

Traction, you see. In this fashion, he stood as if he had two walking sticks as well as being slightly drunk and/or crippled. He moved forward with slow, giant moonwalker steps.

The first three attempts failed. The starboard boot filled with water and Mattie developed a list. The support vessel, his cousin in a rowing boat, took the boot on board and towed Mattie ashore. Running repairs. Push on, was his mantra; push on.

By this time word had spread far and wide. The next Sunday there was another attempt – think the conquest of Everest. Clear weather, no wind. Perfect conditions. A small crowd gathered. The local paper took Mattie's picture. The priest blessed the boots. Prayers.

This time the boots did him proud. He set off to a ragged cheer. Giant step forward, push rod down. Repeat. He worked up a rhythm. Step, push down. Step, push down. Step, push down. Repeat. Repeat. Repeat. The crowd sensed he was going to make it, or die trying. They surged across the bridge to form a welcoming committee on the other bank.

A few tense moments mid-stream on the mighty river. The crowd held its breath. Our hero struggled. Drown or win. Do or die. What drama, what a day out for a little village. Women remembered what they wore on that outing.

He stepped on to dry land and into history. His own small girlfriend rushed forward, the soldier she'd left him for forgotten – but that ship had sailed. Women.

What is it with women and heroes? The world was now his lobster. Form an orderly queue.

Mattie drove a Morris Minor van with a large roof rack and many toolboxes. He always carried a collapsible canvas canoe, securely lashed down. He canoed during his lunch hour, winter and summer, no matter where he was. He was a flask-and-sandwiches man. His canoe design was an advance on the wartime Cockleshell Heroes special commando force, his heroes. He constantly refined his design for a four-bladed paddle to improve efficiency. He also rode a 500cc Triumph motorbike at full speed. His joke was that his bike was mentioned in the Bible: 'Jesus rode in his Triumph across the desert.'

His business was the operation of a low-loader. He took on only difficult and wide loads. This involved much measuring and rough sketching. He liked things that were complicated and difficult. HEAVY HAULAGE, it said on his gate. He carried a tape at all times and measured the things around him constantly.

My father used to go for a quiet pint with him. They were pals. My father knew how wise he was. They were banished to the yard of the pub as he smoked a huge, curved pipe. This required an array of small knives and tools to keep it lit, sometimes even pliers. Clouds of smoke signalled success like the announcement of the election of a new pope in the Vatican. He drank only sherry. No one knew why. He swore by it. 'Mother's milk,' he called it.

He told my father he was unlucky in love and spoke of his lady friend, one of the few women west of the Shannon smaller than himself. His broken heart told him it was the soldier's uniform she'd left him for. Because he could love no other, he gave his life to inventing.

One day my father came home full of news. Mattie was working on a new challenge, navigating the Royal Canal from the Liffey west to the Shannon. This was long before pleasure boating had begun. The canals were decayed and derelict. The basin at Grand Canal quay was known locally as the Forgotten Pond.

I was offered a position as a 'nipper' on what was to be an 'epic attempt'. History called. Think Sherpa Tenzing. My mother said, 'No son of mine is going to sea with that half-mad midget,' and downed tools.

The plan was to buy a lifeboat from a dredger that was being scrapped in the Liffey dockyards. My father knew the man. It was the Dublin way. We'd take it to Mattie's yard and build *accommodation* and a *wheelhouse*. The work was to take one month. I would be paid £1 per week as a *junior rating*. Royal Navy terms were now standard.

The voyage was to take two weeks. On Mattie's arrival at the Shannon, ladies would be invited for pleasure-cruising on the lakes for a short time. Then the vessel was to be burnt, Viking-style, in the middle of the river, as an offering to the gods.

Words turned into action. An ancient lifeboat, 26ft long, clinker-built, timber, was bought for £50 with a

£10 bung for the lads. It was transported on Mattie's low-loader to the yard. We fell to work. I found salt tablets and hard biscuits from the war under the seat. Exciting. The biscuits were tough as rocks but lovely dunked into a nice cup of tea. We were eating history. The vessel was named *Loretta*, after a lady friend.

During the day, when Mattie was out working, I scraped down the hull. The party wall with the old cinema next door allowed me to share intimate moments of ecstasy with a woman loudly confirming approval of her lover's efforts following a shoot-out in which he had saved her from certain death. By the time the boat – sorry – *vessel* was ready I knew every line and every moan of pleasure in the picture. The old yard man thought she was faking it. It sounded good to me.

By the time I was putting the kettle on for our afternoon tea and cake the soundtrack through the wall had turned into flying crockery and screams of 'The bitch, I'll scratch her eyes out!' My mother said, when I was quizzed, 'So unlike the home life of our own dear Queen.' She and her sister went to see the film, to confirm it was filth and the woman was a hussy.

The little engine was stripped down and lovingly rebuilt. It was started to test on the bench, and all agreed it was as sweet as a nut and ran like a sewing machine. No higher praise. Mattie worked on the *superstructure* (plywood cabin) far into the night, listening to the romance and strife next door during the evening show. We never asked him if he felt she was faking it.

Because of the gossip, the yard attracted attention. We had a break-in. Heavies. The usual: tyres, copper, brass, next week's wages. I discovered this when I opened the warehouse and found the two yard Alsatians, Winston and Margaret, hanging dead from ropes twenty-five feet up in the air under broken skylights. The heavies had dropped rope lassoes onto the ground and put meat in the centre. As the dogs ate, they pulled the noose tight and hanged them high. We buried them under a bed of nettles. Mattie, me and the yardman cried.

To get to the yard I had to pass a gang of Teddy boys standing outside the cinema. By this time word had leaked of the attempt and my role in it.

'Is Mattie bringing the other six?' I was asked.

'Will you have women in every town?'

'Are you out or on a message?'

I walked past with my Marmite sandwiches and shouted back, 'I have two big brothers!' It was my mother they should be afraid of. But real Teddy boys at that time were hard men, with razorblades in their lapels.

The big day dawned. Sunday morning. Empty streets. A small convoy set out from the yard to the canal lock for the launch. Mattie, of course, had his own crane. The truck was marked DANGEROUS LOAD.

We arrived at the launch site. The crane and slings were set up. The low-loader was backed into position. The lift began. My job was to remain on board to catch a rope *mid-steam* to secure the *vessel*. Our *provisions* (sandwiches) had been laid out: biscuit tins lined up, rubber bands holding the lids shut. Each was marked Lock 1, Lock 2, Lock 3 etc. I realized I was eating the Mullingar sandwiches. Should I tell Mattie? Would we be able to get food down the country?

When I looked out, we were above the trailer and swinging out over the lock. Much shouting and pointing. The *vessel* slowly, slowly sank below the wall and gently settled on the water. We were afloat. The slings went slack. A wonderful, light-as-air sensation. Mattie beamed with excitement. I was rearranging the Mullingar sandwiches with the Ashtown sandwiches when I felt water lapping at my ankles. I was wondering what this meant when I heard shouts from the quayside.

'You're sinking, you're sinking! Jump for your life!'

I froze. The Ashtown sandwiches fell into the water. The *vessel* was going down fast. I climbed out onto the roof of the *superstructure*. The boat settled on the bottom of the canal at an angle. I was left in the middle of the canal on one square foot of plywood, surrounded by water. I could feel the boat still moving. Tricky. Time for a cool head.

Mattie, ashen-faced, shouted: 'Keep calm, do not move a muscle! I have a plan.'

He jumped into the crane and swung the hook out over me. I grabbed a hold and was hoisted through the air and landed ashore. It was like something in a war movie. My finest hour. If only my pals could see me. Bravest of the brave.

We regrouped.

My mother had heard what was going on and there she was. I tried to explain to her that this was no place or time for a woman and got a clip round the ear in front of my fellow crew members. The shame, the shame.

She pulled Mattie's cap off and threw it into the canal. 'Mad old bastard!' she shouted.

She caught me by the ear, like in the *Beano*, and dragged me home.

'I'm a man,' I said.

'You're a brat,' she said.

Back at home I was put to bed. The doctor was called. 'There's nothing wrong with me!' I shouted down the stairs.

'You're in shock,' she shouted back. 'You may have fleas.'

'My crew need me, I want to stay with my men!' I shouted again.

My father had gone into hiding. This meant he was drinking in a strange pub and might as well be on the moon.

The rest of my story can only be told second-hand. Me and my father were barred from Mattie's yard. For ever.

'Mad dwarf bastard!' she said over and over. 'My beautiful son, left stranded on the sea.'

I tried to explain that the canal was not the sea, and got another clip on the ear.

Poor Mattie salvaged his failed boat alone. He could explain: it was a rotten plank, squeezed by the hoist.

Push on. Fail again, fail better. But there was no push on. No girls in every town.

'Remember the *Titanic!*' the Teddy boys shouted. 'Can Grumpy swim?'

He retired to his yard a broken man. He went back to inventing. He built a huge radio mast and learnt Morse code. He made many new friends around the world. His call sign, or handle, was 'Walk on water'. His new friends would never know from the *dot-dash-dot* streaming across the night skies of the world's oceans that they were dealing with a hero. But I knew, and Mattie knew I knew.

3
WHY DO BEES DANCE?

Hibo was a casual day-labourer who stood waiting for work every morning at the dock gates. If there was no work, a large crowd of men went home with nothing, or went to the dockside pub to drink on the slate. Truckers picked up men to land cargo 'under the hook' from working ships.

I was a boy on school holidays: my job was to drive a pick-up and hire men for our loading. Hibo was a regular and we became unlikely friends. He had a strangeness and sadness in him. He stood apart from the group. He was born into the savage poverty of a 1930s Dublin tenement. He lived on the street, tough and hard as nails. He sang softly or whistled. He rarely spoke.

At sixteen he joined the British army to get away from a violent, murderous father. He went to war and was captured by the Japanese at the fall of Singapore. He spent the war working on the Burma death railway. His job was to bury the dead. If the track was building over stony ground and it was too hard to dig, they burnt a pile of corpses each morning with petrol.

He received many brutal beatings, which happened when a prisoner caught the eye of a guard. All prisoners had to look down when a guard was present. He survived the war, but was damaged physically and hurt spiritually.

When he came home, he lived in the Iveagh lodgings if he had work and the price of a bed. If not, he slept rough winter and summer.

Before the coming of containers, dockside work was hard labour. Cranes landed heavy hoists of sacks and cargo onto trailer beds, to be laid out as a safe load. 'Let the weight do the work,' was the advice. Swing the sack loosely. Lift gently, move slowly, keep a rhythm, keep legs soft and bend. Steady. Never stand under a swinging hoist. Work, watch, wait.

Some Saturday mornings after pay-out I went for a walk with Hibo and his friend John; a ramble, they called it. It was always the same. First port of call – the stones market in Cumberland Street. Second-hand coats and boots sold off the cobblestones. Women fitted and fussed over the men like mothers with small boys. Much coarse laughing. You would not want to be shy or easily shocked. I was asked, was I a virgin? Mary could soften my cough. Have you dropped yet, son. Scarlet.

Next up – the Flying Angel sailors' rest. White-pudding sandwiches and a big mug of hot, sweet tea. Crews from every nation, every colour, every creed. Broken English, sometimes singing, even in the morning. Photos passed around of much-missed families; crowds of children and small, unsmiling women. The odd tear, brown faces twisted in loneliness. Years away at sea, wages sent home to distant villages.

Always, the Liffey ferry across the river to Sir John Rogerson's Quay. The ferryman was a local hero. 'Good-looking women free,' he shouted up, 'pregnant woman down the back.' A good sob story always worked. 'I'll pay you next week.'

'No bother. We know where you live.'

As the ferry set out: 'Bring us back a parrot.'

The steel hull banged hard against the towering granite blocks. Greasy, dangerous, steep steps. It was good to get up to dry land and the warm sun. The river was not to be trusted.

Then a walk to the Iveagh Baths in Tara Street where the *Irish Times* building is now. My friends showed me one of Dublin's secret places. Up and over the pool and its squealing kids, a quiet corridor was lined on each side with doors of dimpled, frosted glass. Each opened into a clean, bare room with a large, deep white bath with heavy brass taps. The man handed out a rough towel and a bar of carbolic soap. He filled the bath to the top with scalding water. There was no chat here. Men sat on wooden benches in the hall, reading in silence. It was a peaceful and private place, the noise of the main pool muffled and far away.

I was too young to be let in so I waited across the street in a café. My friends came out transformed. They were relaxed and happy. It was the high point of their week. I learned many years later that not only poor people used the baths – many professional men went to that calm and secret place.

In the café, before we parted, Hibo and John would tell stories of the war. A British officer, much liked, gave English lessons to Indian troops based on the story of 'Why Bees Dance'. It is because they have done their work well, collected their pollen, and dance and wiggle with happiness and delight. 'A lesson for us all,' the officer would say, 'a lesson for us all.' The whole class did the wiggle dance and never forgot.

Another secret, which shames me to this day. Hibo and John had nowhere to go as the hostel did not open until six o'clock. They would walk to Dalkey or Howth to stay out of the pub and keep their money for the hostel. Meanwhile I went home to my mother for my tea and a warm fire.

School started up again and I did not see Hibo for nearly a year. At Christmas he had failed in health and looked thin and worn.

At home one day my father was upset and agitated. He told us that men would call to the door and we were to stay away. It was Hibo and John who came. They carried a small white box with a dead infant in it. My father drove them to Glasnevin, where they buried the little white box in the angel plot. My father had arranged it with a gravedigger he knew from the pub. All day my mother cried her heart out and clung to me fiercely. She did not let me out of her sight.

A bitter cold winter morning with roads heavily frosted and dangerous. I was opening up the yard for an early start. Along the wall of a warehouse stood a row of heavy timber hogsheads to catch the rainwater from the vast slate warehouse roof. Around one of the hogsheads lay chunks of ice and in it, Hibo, sitting in the water, only his head showing with his cap on, just above the icy water. He had been there most of the night. He stopped his soft singing to wish me good morning. He said it was too hot in the jungle and he was cooling down.

Two older drivers lifted him out of the freezing water. He was naked except for his cap, painfully thin and white as a boy. The men wrapped their coats around him and carried him into the office. He was sat in front of a big electric fire. The medical chest was broken open for the brandy. I made him hot, sweet tea. He told me I was the only person who had ever been kind to him. He told me it was one of the best times of his life when I got him to tell me the dancing bees story over and over because I loved it so much. We did the wiggle dance. My father and a driver put him into warm, dry clothes and brought him in a small van to Grangegorman mental asylum. He was put to bed where he slept for three days and nights.

Some weeks later Hibo started work as a cleaner in the asylum bakery. The old pals act from the pub had got him this plum job. My father called to see him. He said he loved the routine and security, tending the big ovens, happy as a baby. The whole bakery shone with his work.

The following Christmas a package arrived, beautifully wrapped in pristine, heavy brown paper and tied with twine. Government issue. In it were a loaf of bread and a small, plain cake. The note was from Hibo. I knew it was written by another hand, as he could not write.

I am happy for the first time in my life, he said. *I am content and love my work. I have been promoted to trainee baker and this is my first loaf. I will bless each loaf I make for your good fortune. I put my war medal into the little cake. I hope you will remember me when you see it. I hope you will visit me when you are old enough to get in. Bring a white pudding and I will bake bread for a sandwich for you. I hope you will remain my friend.*

He died in the winter of that year. He was buried in an unmarked grave with not one living soul present. He had no family and as we had no official connection to him we were not informed of his death.

Hibo had a hard, cruel life, marked only by a cheap, mass-produced medal he won fighting in a war he did not understand and which had nothing to do with him. But his life touched the hearts of one family. His medal is minded, and the one small photo of him that we have is carefully kept in our biscuit tin. This must make him part of the family, and maybe that's enough.

4
DIPSTICK DAY

Saturday morning, payday. Men looked forward to it. It was not work. It was a gathering of men for men.

An old yard by the river: trucks, cranes, trailers, cargo, workshops. A place of work. An oil drum punched with the square holes of a pickaxe. Timber burning inside. Three more oil drums lashed together in a shamrock shape surrounded by pallet seating for thirty men. Friends and comrades. Each man knew the other. Good and bad, fights forgotten. Friends.

Boiling, blackened kettles, teapots, ancient cracked mugs. Tea leaves in twists of paper, milk in old Baby Power bottles.

Each man shyly put in little packets of sweet cake, a slice or two of apple tart, some biscuits. All to share. Jokes about the wife's cooking. Cigarettes stabbed out, stabbers behind ear. No smoking during eating. Some men took their caps off and put them on their knee, a strange gesture, no longer seen.

Older men wore the jacket of their good suit. They were treated with deference. This was a time to be marked. There was an air of gentleness. Men behaved kindly one to another. Kindly is a strange word to use for men gathered, but kindly it was.

A man took off his boots and pulled out the laces to show a yard boy how to lace his work boots properly and safely. I watched. I repeat it to this day. Knowledge handed down. Those iron-muscled hands could lash down a cargo with secret knots that would endure the storms of seven seas and not stir. Yet they were gentle this day.

Most work was piece-rate and led by the daily port 'read'. No work, no pay. No books. No cheque. No guff. Cash. Nelson Eddies, readies. Saturday morning. Every week.

Each name called out from the office. Each man strode up importantly for his wages. Pride was there. Quick tot agreed. Money slapped down. Silver lined up in little green, red, brown bank bags with little punch holes in the sides. Quick look at the pretty girl in the office. She had more power than she would ever know.

Walk back to fire, money comfortable in pocket. Smiles, I remember, big smiles.

One or two of the men had ramshackle old cars. These were much admired. A star turn in the centre of the yard, always with the bonnet up. It is a truth universally acknowledged that men love looking into an engine. After a wash by many willing hands, it was time for the magic ritual of the oil check. When the oil settled (much discussion of this point) the owner – and only the owner – slowly, dramatically took out the dipstick and displayed it on a clean rag for all to see, its mystery open to the light. The little ogham lines told their secret story. All was well. The matador slid back his sword to fight again another day. A sigh of satisfaction in the group. Job well done. Talk of oil pressure, mileage, icy roads. All conquered. Someday soon they would buy a car, a Ford. Your only man. No nonsense. Would run on the smell of an oily rag.

Fire put out. Sweep yard. Ready to go to pub. Will there be work next week? God is good.

Black, foaming pints bought in rounds, hidden friendships laid down from long before time remembering. The good manners of a new large Player's offered with the clean snap of cellophane and one cigarette eased forward for your friend to take. A small, quick cave of light in cupped hands. Blue words. Fathers nodded to sons, all good, all good.

After the pub, the toss school. A local green space. A hundred men tightly packed. The tosser, Willyboy, with two halfpennies on a small flat stick. Throw into the air, higher than a house. Tumbling, splitting the light. Heads or tails, odds or evens. Win or lose, winner take all. A shouting circle of men formed by outstretched arms, each man holding back the other. Heads back, faces to the sky. Shouting as they fell back to earth. Then, the appalling truth of life laid bare for all to see. It's all random chance. Pure luck or lack of it. Winners shouting, losers silent. Bets paid out. Told you I felt lucky today. It was ever thus. We are all spinning halfpennies in the air, to fall face up or face down. Life.

Then, affection shown by soft punch. A light touch to the elbow. See you Monday. Big ships due in. Plenty of work. But the tidal wave of change was on the sea to sweep away this little world. The halfpennies would fall wrong.

Beware.

5

SMOKO

Hairoil O'Reilly ran a budgerigar-breeding business as a front for his after-hours robbery work.

But it was elegant robbery. His work was careful, considered, measured, but most of all it was highly intelligent, for he was highly intelligent. The Dublin word is 'wide'. Nothing to do with education. He was born wide – wide as a wagon of monkeys, as the saying goes.

He had studied the social order and concluded there was nothing at the so-called top that he did not already have. Posh accents and following orders were not for him. Fur coat, no knickers. Losers; sheep: stick it. He was a main man and all who needed to know, knew. No social climbers here.

Every man of standing in the docks kept a loft and raced pigeons. Fanciers – always loved that word. The lofts were kept like little palaces. Each morning the fanciers stood in a line on the bridge which spanned the main shunting yards that led into the port. Height, you see. The pigeons like it. It worked on natural gravity and followed the gentle contour cradling the city to its river. The main lines formed into hundreds of sidings. Each polished track of old silver slithered to the south in the morning sun.

Two ancient steam locos wheezed all day and mothered the trains into their bays, single wagons rolled silently on the grade. At baby-steps speed. Not a sound. Dangerous. Watch your back. Shunters rode the trains by sticking a long paddle into the axles. They sat on them with legs crossed and glided along, easy as pie on the curving tracks. Not a care in the world. Whistling. It looked like a nice way to spend a morning.

The bridge had a wide parapet and fanciers put their cages of birds up on it. Training for racing was serious. This was a 'smoko'. A time of rest, quietness, no sudden moves, soft talk, man to man. This was the birds' time, and they knew it. Flying in joyous, sunlit circles, soaring out over the river and the morning city and back to a helping hand and a warm nest. Then, when the birds had homed, a quiet smoke – a smoko. This was done after signing on at the labour. Mug money, mickey money. Only fools and horses.

Hairoil had followed his father Brylcreem into the exotic-bird business. Yes, it was funny, but you'd laugh behind your hand. They had an Uncle Shiner. No prizes for guessing why. More hair on a goosegog.

Brylcreem had built up a clientele of rich old and not-so-old ladies from the Southside who collected birds. On Sundays, big cars would wait at the top of his terraced street while the ladies viewed his stock. He took them by the side entrance into his shed – his aviary, as he called it. Notions. The wife was at her mother's on Sunday. Refreshment during business was always a Baby Power by the neck as is traditional and proper. He showed them his exotic wares. Say no more. Another satisfied customer.

Every year he sent the wife and her sisters to Benidorm for a fortnight. Respect. This was the social event of the summer for the whole area. His son kept up the family tradition. It was bringing the sisters that gave the trip its power and magic. Tales of moonlight bingo, karaoke by the pool. Jealous whispers. Presents drew a big silent crowd for the unpacking. Once I got a paper sombrero. Heelball, still have it.

Hairoil had a large notebook and binoculars for his bird training.

'What's in the book?' I asked one day

'There's a front and back,' he said.

'Start at the front,' I said.

'Flying times from France, Holland, Germany ... breeding, training, feeding. We're winners,' he said. 'This is a tough room.'

'And the back?'

'Business,' he said. 'I'll show you. It's in code.' Dense, minute information, rigorous work, cryptic. 'See that line?' he asked. *E.19. x 42. W 4.am*

'What does it mean?'

'I'll tell you,' he said, 'but you have to take it to the grave, or trouble. Understand?'

'Understood,' I said.

'East, track 19, export, con bogie 42, whiskey, Friday,' he said. 'I know every container. The load every week, every shipping cycle, export/import, every weekly manifest,' he said, looking at the sky. 'I like working out plans, logistical resources.'

'You're wasted,' I said. 'You should be running a large corporation.'

'People like me don't get to run things.'

'How would you get a container out of here?' I asked. 'They must weigh twenty tons.'

'Twenty-three point seven,' he said. 'Did you ever get a puncture? Did you use a jack to lift the car? Did you ever see a big-truck jack? They lift thirty tons. They go under any load. Bottle jacks, they're called.'

'I didn't know that.'

'Listen and learn,' he said. 'Foggy night. *Match of the Day*. Liverpool. Fake roadworks here. Fencing, vans, gear. Four-man team goes down a Jacob's ladder blacked out like the minstrels.'

'Jacob's ladder?'

'Rope ladder with timber steps. Pilots go up them to get onto ships at sea.'

'Right,' I said. 'Simple.'

'Not simple,' he said. 'We don't do simple.'

'What are minstrels?' I asked.

'The Black and White Minstrels. White men blacked up to sing mammy songs. An old TV show still loved around here.'

A favourite story, told and retold. Lino, an old docker watching, said, 'By Jaysus them blacks can sing.'

'Why Lino?' I whispered in Hairoil's ear.

'He's always on the floor.' His brother Rolo was fond of sweets. Easy.

Check container number from my 'notes'. Open front twist locks. Put jacks under corners. Pump. Container will tilt slowly to three feet off bed of rail bogey. Two small strong men get under with silent electric saw. Carefully cut floorboard. Cases of whiskey will come into view. Create human chain. Convey cases to bridge. Lift with mobile electric hoist, twenty cases a lift. Put into vans, leave quietly. Replace floorboards carefully and reseal. Clean whole area spotless. Not a mark. Silence. Total silence.

'Why Liverpool?' I ask.

'People round here think Croke Park is for culchies. It's only up the road. This was an English garrison port. We still do the pools, read English page-three-girl papers, watch soccer. Love Liverpool, love Liverpool. COME ON YE REDS!' he chanted. 'Not a man in that control tower will be sober or take his eyes off the telly during the match. He will shout till hoarse, we would be seen quicker on the moon.'

A pigeon landed. 'That's Mussolini,' he said.

I laughed out loud with delight. The pigeon had the stiff, short legs and self-important strut. He had a puffed-up chest. It was uncanny. All he needed was a row of tiny medals. His malicious eye sought for any imagined slights. Perfect, perfect, perfect.

Months passed. Sitting in Bewley's café skimming the papers. 'Mystery in Yokohama'. Irish container empty on arrival, ship's captain questioned. Seal intact in Dublin, Japanese mafia blamed. Fake seal scam.

The next day I went to the bridge.

'How's Mussolini?' I asked.

'Dead.'

'Jesus.'

'Serves him right,' he said. 'He wasn't winning. Too much showing off. Hawk got him.'

'Yokohama?' I asked.

'The Nips had a good day,' he said. 'I hear they like whiskey.'

I was silent. Poor Mussolini.

'I want to show you something,' he said. He opened the diary at the back, the business end. 'In two weeks, a special load is on its way.'

'What's in it?' I asked.

'Old used notes for incineration.'

'How much would there be,' I said.

'Fifteen million,' he said.

'Fifteen million?' I said.

'Fifteen million,' he said.

There was a long silence.

'I'm looking for a partner,' he said. 'Straight down the middle: 60–40.' No one laughed at the old joke.

'A quiet pint?' he asked. 'Rollicking Biddy's?'

Biddy was a man. Old school tough: no fighting, no biting, no crisps, no credit. Biddy's was a singing house. Strict protocols, Saturday night only. Noble call by Mrs Mac, a lion tamer. Each man, woman, child got a turn. No coaxing. All knew the words and did their best. All got a round of applause and respect. At the end of the night, three songs belted out by the whole house. Crowd-pleasers. And always last, the house favourite: a hurtin' song, a cheatin' song. A woman who wronged her man. Delilah. Who but 'Delilah'? The crowd leaned into the pain, into the hurt. Wishing it away. *'Why, why, why?'* The women knew.

Then: 'Have you no house to go to?' bawled out. The open swallow of the last pint. But no child ever went without new shoes for First Communion if money was tight in a house. Every little girl was asked for a twirl in her new frock. A half-crown each. Any man who beat his wife would feel those iron fists. A man's man. Earrings optional.

Biddy had gone to sea at fifteen, as local men did at the time. Before containers that meant deep sea, blue water. Two years sign on, ship out. He did well. Bosun. Top wages, could lead men. Came home with tidy savings and bought the old pub. Lived upstairs. Had friends but never married. This was quietly accepted: every cripple has his way to crawl.

On a quiet afternoon he would potter behind the bar in a ladies' blouse with a string of pearls, sometimes mascara, always gold earrings and perfume. Never a word said, not a dicky. Your private life is your own. When he did this, sailors showed their tattoos when tattoos were still mysterious. Seamen then could sew, knit, weave, make and mend. Life at sea made them neat and tidy. Shipshape, Bristol fashion. You could see it in them, the way they stood.

Then a ship would be into a foreign port for weeks as cargo was worked by hand from deep between decks by coolie labour. Time to read and write letters. These men were different. They had friends in Japan, Vietnam, Spain. They could set a table properly.

In the snug. Little hatch. Small doors closed. Business being done, men at work. Manners cost nothing. Morning sun outside peeping in as it should be. Two black pints settling nicely, staring up at us. Lovely.

'Well,' he said.

'Here's to Mussolini,' I said. 'Which way does the 60–40 go?'

6
NOT ONLY PIGEONS FLY

Hairoil had been a busy boy. An hour in the morning with his racing pigeons, then a sandwich in the snug of Rollicking Biddy's with Biddy and a small group of men. Fierce, quiet, intense conversation. No notes. No paper. No record. No outsiders. No flash. No mercy. No quarter. To the grave.

Work far into the night. Drive to random distant phone boxes. Never use the same one twice. Driver carries heavy bag of coins.

Away a lot. Travel alone as always. Boat to Liverpool, then who knows. No booking, no name, no ticket, no passport. No record. Anorak, clean jeans, good boots polished. A tidy brickie going to work in England like his father before him. Blend in, head down. Use the loaf, think. Think hard. Every move weighed and measured. Like it says in the book: silence, exile, cunning.

Pre-dawn, winter morning. Mister Sun wonders is there any point in getting out of bed. Foot-stamping time. Mister Frost has done his work. Mister Snow is making up his mind and it's not looking good.

A vast floodlit transport yard, glittering with cold, setting up, ready for the day's work. Heavy diesel engines snorting as they're kicked awake. The slap as tractor units are slammed into trailers. The fifth-wheel mechanism locking the three-inch pin onto the large greased plate. The fifth wheel: that's what makes trucks bendy.

Drivers and yardmen speak quietly beneath staccato bursts of cigarette smoke, blue as blue in the arc lights. 'Queenie, 3.30 pm, Chepstow, on the nose,' into his ear.

Phitchoo, phitchoo, phitchoo. The trailer's air brake chambers fill as the suzies are connected from the cab to the trailer. The bright spirals of red, yellow and blue carry electrics and air to the trailer brakes. Check next time you are beside a big truck in traffic. Now you will know what you are looking at.

Today's job is to load a tanker ship with a million pints of Guinness. Non-haz, strict hygiene, human consumption, twenty-four tons per load. Ten tractor-tankers start at 6 am sharp, finish at noon to catch the tide. Two thousand five hundred tons, sign here please, job done. Except it isn't, not that day. Not that day.

The tanker trailers are slim, polished silver tubes lying at a slight angle. Razzle-dazzle in the sun. Six fat black tyres on silver chrome wheels, Michelin men in blackface. They had been freshly steam-cleaned for the job, and are pure as a young nun. You could eat your dinner off them. Cleaning cert, check. Sealed clean hoses, check. Lights, check. Brakes, check. Fuel, check. Oil and water, check.

Tickety-boo.

Clipboard back on office-wall hook. The ten tractor-tankers lined up down the middle of the yard. Engines running, cabs warm and snug, waiting for barrier to lift. Hold on a mo – message from office. Four government hygiene inspectors will travel today. Snap inspection to check the safety and loading protocols.

Black minivan pulls into yard, four men in white boiler suits get out with briefcases, wearing hygiene masks and baseball hats. The senior man goes into the office and presents his official letter to the yardman.

'Department of the Environment hygiene officer,' he says. 'Shouldn't take more than two hours. You're our star client, best in the business. We won't get in the way, and when we come back we'll bring fig rolls for a nice cup of tea. Do up my report. Sign here please.'

Mrs Kelly in the office, long-married, but still she sees he has a nice bottom in the white boiler suit. It really *is* white. 'When a mummy cares, it shows,' said the old ad before the pictures started.

'All in order, see you soon with the fig rolls.' He gives Mrs Kelly a smile. Ooooooh.

He and his men get into four tractor units. Security barrier lift, trucks move slowly out into the busy morning traffic. Headlights blink hello to mates in trucker code: the rules of the road mean something different down here. They follow the Liffey up to the loading station.

Trucks split up under silos. Still dark, but bright as day in the loading yard. Another blast of steam to ensure clean. The yard inspector breaks the seal, opens the rear valve and signals that loading can commence. A lab technician takes samples in small bottles all along the line.

The government inspectors sit in cabs writing notes and walkie-talkie-ing to each other. They are not friendly, there is no chat. It's official business. 'Sorry, no, I can't tell you where I live, no, I'm not married.' Loose lips sink ships.

A half-hour of six-inch hoses, humping to rhythm, as product is pumped from silo to tankers. Flow gently, Sweet Afton. Automatic cut-off when full. Twenty-four tons exactly. Two men, sideways twist to release valve. Steam hose to clean down connection. Hygiene cover snapped on. Sign here please.

Driver into cab, drives to gate of complex. Gently eases out into the traffic. All ten tankers are now going down the quays to port and spreading out along the route.

Government officials sitting with briefcases on lap. At 8.15 am precisely all cases open, walkie-talkie squawks loud: all four tankers with inspectors are to stop immediately due to an emergency. All four drivers brake hard and stop dead in heavy morning traffic. Immediately, angry horns start blaring.

Government official takes pistol out of briefcase and holds it to driver's head. 'Pull right across all lanes of traffic now or you're a dead man.'

All drivers do as told. Front of tractor units up near Liffey wall with trailer blocking all traffic. Bedlam. Government official takes keys out of ignition and throws into river. He takes heavy steel canister from briefcase and puts on dashboard.

'This is cyanide gas,' he says, 'pre-set release by remote control. I'm getting out now and if you move or open the door it will release and you will die instantly and in agony, as will as all surrounding persons. Give me your phone.'

Throws phone into river.

'Put your hands on wheel.' Handcuffs driver's wrist to wheel. 'Do not touch canister or door for three hours, then you will be safe. Understand? Tell the police not to open the door.'

'Yes I will,' says driver, eyes wide with terror. The government official gets out of the cab. Cuts suzies and hits connectors hard with a hammer. All brakes lock solid. This truck will take hours to move. All four trucks are the same, across all main arterial crossroads.

It takes thirty minutes for the city to come to a stop. People get out of cars to see what's happening. Distant police sirens wail to no avail into the deafening horn-blowing. Tailbacks stretch up the Naas Road and airport road. People lock cars and leave them.

Government officials walk away and melt into crowd.

A separate, empty silver tanker has parked in Dame Street, opposite Trinity and in between the two bank head offices. The driver goes up the inspection ladder and opens all top hatches. He takes four big boom-boxes and puts them on the ground facing in four different directions. He switches them on. He places heavy steel canisters beside them. A huge amplified voice fills the square; a distorted, metallic, foreign accent.

'You are witnessing the biggest bank raid in history. You will not be hurt if you do as we say. Do not approach this area. These canisters contain cyanide. They will activate on movement sensors and many people will die in agony.'

The message keeps repeating, on and on and on and on and on.

The driver unhitches the tractor unit out from the trailer and parks at the Trinity gates. He fires a flare into the cab, which bursts into a huge fireball. Dense black smoke rises into the morning sky. A head appears from the open top hatch of the silver tanker and a man climbs out onto the catwalk. He is followed by seven others. All wear white overalls, hygiene masks, hats and gloves and carry large toolboxes.

They split into two groups and four move to each bank precisely at 10 am as doors open. They walk in with the public. They place large boom-boxes on the counters, switch them on: same message, same voice. Loud. Loud. Very loud. They place six canisters along the counter and order staff to assemble. They ask for the two senior managers to step forward. They tell them the cyanide cylinders are primed to release in forty-five minutes' time: anyone still in the building or within a hundred metres will die instantly.

'I want every safe opened immediately and every safe deposit box opened with the master key. I want your staff to help us load these hundred large canvas sacks. Anyone who does not work will be shot dead.'

In one bank, the manager says, 'I can't do that.'

The official shoots him between the eyes, his head snaps back. Official turns to assistant manager. 'Did you hear my instructions, do you need them repeated? You have ten seconds.'

The assistant manager turns to the assembled staff: 'Open all safes and boxes and help to load sacks immediately, then leave the building when finished. This is an official order.'

The work begins. As each waterproof sack is filled it is carried out of the banks into the street, up the trailer ladder and dropped down hatch into empty tanker. The work is methodical, there is no speaking. The boom-boxes continue their frightening message. The man on the catwalk throws down the sacks from both banks. Not a word, not one single word.

After thirty minutes the tape changes. It says: 'We need to pick up the speed.' The noise reverberates off the building, the staff toil hard and look at their watches. Women sob but work. After forty minutes the boom-boxes stop. Heart-stopping silence over the square. Crowds are moved well back, all sirens off. Quiet as a grave. Bad-tempered seagulls let their annoyance be known.

In both banks, all staff are told to take off their jackets, lie down on their sides and use jackets as pillows. 'It will be over soon,' the boom-box said. Some staff are so stressed they actually fall asleep.

The eight officials walk out to the tankers, take off all gloves, hats, overalls, masks, shoe-covers and place them all in a large pile in the street. One man fires another flare into the pile and the lot goes up with a whoop of flame. Then all eight men lie on the ground, face down, in the total silence of the deserted street, the only noise the crackling of the tractor unit still burning.

Within a minute, the distant *whop whop whop* of heavy rotor blades. Two massive, double-rotor, black military helicopters come up the street at roof height. Ear-crushing noise crashing off buildings. Crowds scatter and run for their lives. First chopper hovers over tanker. Heavy lifting tackle lowered. Man on catwalk closes hatches. He connects tackle to pre-set shackle on top of trailer.

Chopper and trailer rise slowly from the square. Rotor-wash smashing off elegant Georgian façades. Man on catwalk climbs up, lifting tackle and into chopper. Slow banking turn as trailer rises and sails down centre of Westmoreland Street, then turns east downriver and heads to the port and the open sea beyond. Second chopper lowers two ladders and eight men climb up. It too banks away and follows the river to the sea, leaving a deafening silence behind.

Then boom-boxes start again: 'All trailers booby-trapped with cyanide gas, do not approach, all computers and radars in the city have been corrupted and scrambled. Do not enter square for two hours. Repeat, do not enter, do not enter.'

The city sits and waits. At one o'clock an armoured car enters the square. Inside, a four-man army team in gas masks. Public announcements on radio: all car drivers to turn and go home – the city is closed for the day. Streets clear with full curfew. Heavy army presence on street, armoured cars stop and soldiers begin a search. Chatter on radio, 'It's the Russians, the mafia, the IRA, the Latvians.'

Both choppers follow the river to the sea, right down the middle. Silver trailer gleaming in the sun. A hundred feet up. An amazing sight. Crowds stare in silent disbelief. The image is beamed all over the world. Thirty miles out to sea, choppers turn due south. Thirty miles off Wexford coast, silver tanker is lowered gently into the sea. It sinks quietly, no fuss. Choppers turn east and head to an old Soviet submarine base on the Baltic. The sea settles and closes ranks as it always does: the sea can keep a secret.

Twenty-one days later a heavy old Dutch salvage tug shoulders its way up the Irish Sea in a Force Eight gale. Tough as old boots, a bruiser. Registered around the world many times. On survey mission with a crew from every corner of the earth. During the night it holds station in one spot. When the storm passes, four divers go over the side and a heavy lighting rig is lowered down with them. The trailer lies in a hundred feet of water, on its side. Hatches are opened and unloading starts. A hundred heavy waterproof sacks come to the surface. A winch is lowered and the bags are brought up, four at a time.

As dawn breaks, the job is finished and the tug heads east to the Baltic. One week later, as per contract, each member of a twenty-man military team receives €1 million into a numbered bank account. No names, no pack drill. They never meet or speak again.

The government announced that security had not been breached: a lie. The government says the robbers got away with €30 million: another lie, it was multiples of that. The diamonds, gold and bonds did not surface on the black market for years. What was in the safe-deposit boxes will never be known. The police said they were following a definite line of inquiry: another lie.

Hairoil and his fellow fanciers watched the trailer flying down the Liffey while they trained their pigeons. They took pictures of it with them all firmly in the frame, in that place, at that time. Later, in the snug of Rollicking Biddy's, Hairoil allowed himself one joke. Not only pigeons fly.

7
RUSTLING AT
UNDERNOSE FARM

Hairoil burnt his notes. Carefully, one page at a time. He crumbled the ashes into a glass of slops. Torn-up notes could be put back together. Prying eyes. Not good. Could all end in tears. Secrets are secret. The rest is silence.

Sitting in his head office, the snug of Rollicking Biddy's. The owner, Biddy, his lifelong friend and mine, a sailor home from the sea. 'Do not disturb' in Hairoil's eyes. Men at work.

He was reviewing his vast criminal business. New direction, endgame. Quiet, fierce intelligence, concentration, line by line, man by man, deal by deal. Shaking out weaknesses, testing the machine, probing, sifting, smelling the air, settling scores. Two men would die. Business is business, it would be soon. Calls made. Same routine, randomly chosen public payphones, no mobiles, no computers, no paper, no strangers, cash, dirty cash, long, long chain of command. Please do not touch the goods.

He sat back and took a break. Looked forward to tomorrow's treat. Once a month he and Biddy took two lines of the finest, purest cocaine. Never more, never less.

They went to the zoo, as always. In a battered old van, ex-P&T, bright orange, quiet laugh. To see their old friend Charlie, Cheeky Charlie. Charlie knew them well. They loved him dearly. He had a tyre hanging from a rope. He looped one arm into the tyre like a man leaning on a bar counter. Relaxed like. He crossed his legs down low at the ankles. He looked them in the eye, fair and square. *How are things in Glocca Morra?* he seemed to say. *Turned out nice.* A steady, strong, manly gaze. Not a bother on him. A man's man. One of our own. A pal.

Then the drum-roll moment. Biddy lit a cigarette – Charlie liked Rothman's – and handed it to him through the bars. Charlie took the fag daintily. Quick look to ensure it was properly lit. Took a slow, reflective drag, the cigarette held at the edge of his big dry lips. Eyes half closed. A shiver of pleasure passed among the group. Then the best. He cupped the cigarette in his hand and nonchalantly put it behind his back and resumed his gaze. Not piercing, but searching, open, honest, assured, respectful. They had taught him to do this years ago, as they used to do when they were boys, with a gang of pals, standing at street corners. 'Charles', as it said on the sign on the cage, placed the cigarette on his thumb and with two fingers flicked it back to them. Like all the best laughs in school, they could not laugh out loud. It would be rude, might cause offence. Inside, they screamed. Charles demanded and got respect and, from his point of view, the courtly and formal ritual of a friend's visit had been observed with dignity and style. All in order. No need for bananas. The whole ape enclosure was paid for by a benevolent fund in Jersey. The guard went for his tea when he saw them, if you follow my drift. The funds were from a Bahama lawyer's office with nominee directors. Say no more.

On to an old country pub on the banks of the Liffey. Sitting out in the little yard over the river, settled in nicely.

'Two nice pints, please, and two sausage sandwiches.'

'Certainly,' said the old lady who ran the pub. 'Lovely to see you again.'

'You're looking well,' Hairoil said. 'I hear you're getting engaged.'

'You're an awful man,' she said. 'Who'd have me?'

'I hear you're a snug woman with twenty-five grand in the post office. I'd say you are a catch, and great legs too. I might have an interest myself.'

'The last time I saw twenty-five was on a bus,' she said. 'I had a young man once, I loved him beyond reason and into madness. He went to their stupid war and never came back. I could never look at another.' The pale morning light trembled with her sadness.

She went to make the sandwiches. Silence tiptoed. The river moved on. The drugs coursed their golden magic. They sat together as happy as a man could be. Blissful.

'Lucky men,' Hairoil said.

'Lucky men,' Biddy said.

A gentle elbow in the ribs. A chuckle.

The old lady came back with a tray. Lovely creamy pints, fresh batch bread, four fat sausages smiling.

'Heaven,' said Biddy. 'Where would you get it?'

'Put a horn on a corpse,' Hairoil said.

Old, long-practised patter, a little word-canter. Old friends at ease. It continued.

'Are you a mustard man, yourself?' Biddy asked.

'Ah no, the mammy had me ruined with the red ketchup. "Get it into you son," she said. I told her, "You're a desperate woman."'

He bit into his sandwich. The taste exploded and soared in his mouth, while the pure cocaine drove pulsing delight to every fibre of his body. The old lady felt the silence and the slow chewing of her strange customers and went back to the shadows of her little kitchen. Her lost young lover stood beside her. She cried where they could not see her, her tears running over her old hands. She cursed God and damned her soul.

She would never know that the younger man out in the yard owned the pub and had been looking after her for years. She was told that the rent freeze was due to a legal issue over title. Not her problem, her solicitor said, say nothing. She said nothing. The law is an ass.

They gave her a big tip and told her they had done well on a job as small builders. They said they would be

48

back soon, for a child's big communion party, take over the place for the day.

'Keep a dance for me,' said Hairoil.

'You're too kind,' she said. 'Your van looks banjaxed. I hope if we get married, you'll do better than that.'

'My other car is a Jaguar,' said Hairoil. 'I will strew your path with rose petals on the way to our nuptial couch. We will lie as one among the stars.'

'Are you sure you don't need anything before we go?' he asked. 'You know we love your place. I might propose to you next time, so stay away from handsome men till I get back.'

They both saw her red eyes, and knew. She waved to them all the way up the winding river road as they drove away in their little orange van.

Men, what are they like? she asked herself.

. . . .

Strange days indeed. I was standing at the gate of our yard when a young boy spun around on his new chopper.

'Hey, mister, Stab the Rasher wants to see you in Biddy's,' he said. 'Quiet pint.'

'Cheeky pup,' I said, 'Tell him I'll be round in an hour.'

'Tell him yourself, big shot. Where's my tip?'

I had known Hairoil all my life, but I was never seen with him. I got a turkey at Christmas with no note. I nodded to him when we met.

I went to Biddy's, into the snug. Hairoil and Biddy were waiting. No drinks. A small screen open in front of them. Sunlight fell on rows of sparking glasses.

'Our relationship is about to change,' he said. 'I have tracked you for many years.'

'I greatly admire you and your work. It would be an ambition one day to be your partner in a new life,' he said.

The pub was empty, a woman sweeping. Everything spotless. I said nothing.

'I want to show you this,' he said.

He flicked the screen. It showed a group of wild young boys racing sulky ponies flat out along a busy motorway, heavy traffic backed up behind. It had become a notorious image when talking heads on TV spoke of the breakdown of society. Spread out across the lines of traffic, the long whips singing out to frenzied ponies pulling lightweight chariots with bicycle wheels. It caused a sensation. A big country sergeant waffled on the telly. Outrage, etc. Nothing happened. Funny that.

'Some of those ponies where mine,' Hairoil said. 'Stolen from my farm. Stolen from me.'

'You have a farm?' I said. 'Where is it?'

'That's what I want to talk to you about,' he said. Nothing would surprise me, but I was wrong.

'I want to bring you for a little drive,' he said.

The three of us walked out and got into one of his many vans. This one read 'Maureen: Wedding Dresses,

Home Fittings, Satisfaction Guaranteed for the Fuller Figure, Paris-trained'. Droll. Our boy was always droll.

We drove to his shed behind our main yard. The policeman on the corner carefully studied the house opposite.

Into the shed. Like all his places, it was spotless. A row of vans. Plumbers, roofers, hearing aids, a few good, plain cars, nothing flash. Never flash. A door at the back. Steep stone steps down. Another door. Chilly. Opened into a new world.

A beautifully built vaulted ceiling, good brick, Dolphin's Barn Dublin brick. A 200ft-long curved roof, fully lit, above row after row after row of cages containing every type of bird. Budgies, singing birds, parrots, linnets. I was in shock.

'My party piece,' he said, 'in honour of my father, a well-known bird man. He was fond of you.'

He slid back the little curtain on a big cage. An old parrot blinked into the light. Hairoil rang his nail along the bars and whistled softly.

'Two pints of larger and a packet of crisps please,' said the parrot. 'How's your belly for a lodger, missus?' Then a cackle. Haroil gave the bird a peanut and slowly closed the curtain. Show over. Short and sweet. Call my agent.

'I've been trying to tell you for years,' he said. 'There's more.' Boy, was there more. We walked to the back wall. A large hole had been opened in the Victorian brickwork. I stepped through and into another world. It sounds corny, but I could not believe my own eyes.

Three huge vaulted caverns stretched away into the distance, directly under our yard, each lined with white-painted pens and a central walkway. Looped cable carried bare bulbs. Sheep, goats, ponies, dogs and litters of pups, hens, turkeys, grazing and feeding peacefully. A full working farm, right under the city. Overhead, a modern air-handling system pumped fresh air. Everything clean and proper, as always with Hairoil. He saw me looking up.

'I took it from a computer factory I bought,' he said. From him, that could mean anything.

We walked slowly down through the farm to the end wall, passing by livestock, hay bales, men sweeping.

I heard a noise, growing louder. Now I could not believe my ears. It was the propellers of a ship mooring outside. We were just below the river. Like in a submarine movie, every sound carried in the water.

I gazed at the wall in amazement. When I looked down, a goat was carefully nibbling my hat where I held it in my hand. The ship reversed her screws so that the noise was deafening as she came alongside.

When the noise died away, Hairoil said: 'I love the madness of it. I found it years ago when I was searching for a leak in the floor of my father's budgie business. It started out as a joke, it just grew. Part of the fun was that you did not know, never mind the culchie cop outside. I knew you would like it. You and me.'

'We can't be partners,' I said, 'You're a crim and I'm a five eight.'

'I'm going to be a five,' he said. 'I've sold my international drug operation. My raiding team is disbanded and paid off. Rich man every one. Pensions. There are new days coming. The new rock venue down the road will bring many new people down here didn't know our world existed. The millions of shares I bought for pennies in early tech companies years ago bring in more money that I can spend in a hundred lives. There's no point in robbing. It's all clean now. We should go into the property business, you and me. Open up the docks. Partners, straight down the middle, 60–40. Old joke, I couldn't resist.

'I can't control the young guys anymore,' he went on. 'The smartest ones know the world is loaded against them, with their accents and this address. Even if they do go to school, they'll only end up in front of a screen in a faceless open office with hundreds of other mugs. Drive an hour and a half to a cheap crappy house in an estate with a fake name. To spend their lives paying a mortgage. They know the bullshit guff words, *mission statement, customer service, team-building, Q4,* guff to make gobshites feel important. It's a con job. No way José, the real winner sits by a pool in California reading philosophy and shooting grouse in Scotland in season before wintering in the south of France. "Nice bit of tweed, my lord." They carry guns. They're not afraid. They know the score. My day is done. The fives will win because they rob honestly.'

'You cannot carry on now that I've seen this,' I said.

'I know.'

'Open it to the public,' I said, 'it would be a tourist magnet. A gold mine.'

'You don't get it,' he said. 'It was never about money. It was for you. It's the madness of it. That would be gone. It would be Disney. Americans in yellow trousers looking for the T-shirt shop. "Have you any leprechauns?" I'll close it down, I need six months.'

'No drugs, no stolen goods on the premises,' I said.

'My word,' he said.

'That'll do,' I said.

'Will you be my partner in the new world coming down here?' he asked. 'Clean as a whistle.'

'No,' I said. That *no* cost me uncountable millions.

They asked me back to Biddy's for a pint. I said no.

Six months later to the day, as promised, three of us stood in the middle of our main yard. A fifty-ton road-breaker punched into the ground with a shuddering *rat-a-tat-tat*. A huge hole appeared. The machine was stopped. We all stood around the hole and looked down into that beautiful model farm, all pens swept out and empty, row after row. The first light of heaven in a hundred and fifty years poured down on this bizarre and beautiful work of art. One man took out his phone.

'Take a photo and I'll break both your legs,' Hairoil said. 'It was built after the Famine by the Protestants to feed the poor. It was called Undernose Farm. The health and safety man wants it closed.' They did not get the joke, but I did.

'That's funny,' I said. 'Undernose Farm, that's funny.'

It took six days to fill it up with gravel and rubble. We had destroyed a masterpiece. I never got a bill.

One year later I was stuck in traffic. A black limo stopped outside the new twenty-storey Bank of Arabia. My man got out. Pinstriped suit, snowy-white shirt, pink tie, dainty pumps, the works. A beautiful blonde PA carried papers. He clocked me, walked over to my car.

'Undernose Holdings have already bought fifteen large sites along the river. They have doubled in value already. The banks are raining money down on me. Come to Saudi with me tomorrow. Change your mind. I tell all my new friends I have known you all my life. They are impressed. You have the magic dust I will never have. People like you, they don't like me. They fear me. Come to Saudi, they are sending a private jet.'

The policeman on the corner gave a little salute and a smile. Hairoil and I looked at each other. The wolf was in the fold. Christ in heaven help them.

'I will put something special in the turkey this year,' he said. You'll never guess what it was.

Weeks later, I went to the zoo. I was first in. I went straight to Charlie's cage, or should I say Charles'. He was sitting against the back wall, legs stretched out. He seemed to have aged. Do gorillas look old or young? He did not know me. He yawned, a huge yawn. We looked at each other for half an hour, in silence. I felt like saying, Hairoil and Biddy send their regards.

To me he was a slightly puzzled old man who had gone for a little doze and woken up to a changed world. I know the feeling. I had brought a banana. When he saw it he came to me with his Teddy-boy shuffle, shoulders held high. He peeled it slowly and ate it with relish, but nicely. He politely handed me back the skin and held his ground.

But I had a plan.

Thank you, Charles. I will name my new company after you, Charles Holdings Ltd. You will be the richest gorilla in Dublin. No, not a pinstripe. Perhaps a dressy dark blue. Classy. But pink? Never. Never. I'm a pinstripes man. Charles nodded his approval. We would look after business, Charles and I.

8
WIDOWS' MEMORIES

Allow me to introduce my gang of four. A fine body
of men. First up, The Little Flower, a good scrapper.
Fears no man. Age: fourteen years. The Prof, yes,
you got there before me: thick as plaited pig shit. But
sometimes he said things that swayed and shimmered
in the air and brought a silence. Then Skin: more meat
on a butcher's pencil. Courage of a lion. Age: fourteen
years. Snag: smart, smart and cunning, a good planner,
our second-in-command. Officer material. Age: fifteen-
and-a-half years. Then there's yours truly. Leader. El
Supremo. A looker. All-round good egg. Age: fourteen-
and-a-half years.

We were meeting in central HQ, a huge old 1950s
American Chevrolet dumped at the bottom of my dad's
yard. Overgrown with nettles. Good camouflage in the
event of surprise attack. Deep leather back seat, squeaky
springs. Lovely old smell on a sunny day. My uncle Joe,
with the club foot, known to one and all as Hopalong,
ran it as a taxi during the war. I used to try on his special

boot. Nice. A rich American woman once gave him a £25 tip. Fond of the ladies, our Joe. A charmer. Runs in the family.

Our meeting was held with us all piled on top of each other on the big back seat. Boys like this. It's called a scrag. There was plenty of room in the front but it was never used. It was for guests only, our good room, mind the ornaments.

The yard and our Chevrolet hideout was on the riverfront at the old port. It was surrounded by stacked cargo and trailers, facing south, a sun trap.

One famous day the gang were in among the nettles on a carpet, an old Persian rug from my granny's good room, taking the air. There was a high spring tide and the river was nearly up to the top of the wall. Fast-ebbing, swollen, dangerous.

Suddenly a seal. Curved scimitar back as they do, a crescent moon. Floating on his back, relaxed as a deckchair. Half-eaten salmon under his flipper. Lunch. He saw us as we saw him. Twelve eyes locked in a primal stare. His gaze told of mild interest, gentle and slightly puzzled. He sailed swiftly past on the tide, his fish forgotten. He was our friend from that moment, our guiding star. The Day of the Seal. Don't worry. Be happy.

It was a slack day. Short agenda. We were on a comic-reading break. Sharing a borrowed Woodbine. Three drags per man, don't Bogart the joint.

Then Prof said one of his things. 'Why don't we save up and plan a big day out? Do all our favourite outings and finish with a blowout?' Altogether, comics down, pondering, nodding, murmurs of approval, lips moving in calculations.

I immediately took command. I know my men.

'How much are we talking here,' I asked.

'Two-and-six per man,' he said. This has to be money no object. The world's our lobster.

Snap-decision time. 'Let's do it,' I said. Leader. El Supremo.

The meeting came to life. All ideas were put forward. Serious stuff. Debating, yes, no, maybe. One idea: we would go to the Spanish gypsy woman who worked at the corner of Misery Hill. Fierce row, idea was shot down. We were too young. She was old, some said nearly thirty. She'd take all our money. She was a bit frightening. She could only pick one of us to be her 'companion'. She had a sister, bit of a dog. Trap six, Harold's Cross. But what about the others? Equality, as the Frogs say, one for all.

Finally, a day's programme of events emerged. It was unanimous.

1. Bus stop 9 am sharp.
2. Pool money in the special sock. I would be bag man, of course.
3. Bring chocolate. You're not you when you're hungry.
4. Visit our old friends the shrunken heads.
5. Shake the hand of the Dead Nun.
6. Go to penny dinners. Blag in. Discuss tactics.

7. Visit 100-ton crane. Review plan for entry.

8. Broadway caff. Blowout. Tightener.

And so it came to pass the following Saturday.

On bus, as usual pay three fares: the other two are 'special needs'. Good acting. Practice makes perfect. One woman makes the sign of the cross. 'Their poor mother,' she says. All piled into one seat. Good scrag.

Into the museum. Celtic crosses, boring. Early manuscripts, boring. Chalices, boring. History stuff, boring. Third floor, glass case at the back. Our three pals. Lovely. They smile when they see us, their little orange faces the size of a child's fist. Twinkly eyes that follow you round the room. Long black shiny hair like John Rocha. They look in good humour, even cheerful in difficult circumstances. A little smile as we leave. They know – they just know – that they are much loved. 'See you next Tuesday,' to the guard.

Read instructions on how they are made. First catch a person you don't like. Behead. Cut the top of skull off. Empty contents. Fill with hot stones. Lovely. Keep up the hot-stones process over three months. Hang in smoky tent for twelve months. Love it. Life today is dull. Beheading frowned upon. No hot stones. Wash your hands. Nicely nice. No wonder crime has soared. Bring back beheading, I say.

Back on the street. Next up St Michan's. Walk along quays to Four Courts. Crowds of Americans out in front. Tourists are a nuisance. They should be banned. In and down the clammy steps. Sudden cold and dark.

Torch waving at end of long black corridor.

'Don't step on a coffin,' says the torch.

'What, in these shoes?' I say, an old line, I know.

Echoes, intense cold, not good. You don't want to be a big girl's blouse down here.

Heavy, rusted-steel gate. One weak bulb. Coffins propped against wall. Lids thrown back. One long brown leather person. Looks like sleeping off fourteen pints. Bad pints. Next, a midget leather thing. The nun. Outstretched shiny, tiny hand. Polished, long black dirty nails, claws like a rat's. Suggestive leer from ear to ear, except there are no ears. As leader, I put my hand in first. I looked into the vacant sockets. Fear. Each man in turn then flees to the little square of blessed sunlight splashed on the cruel stone floor.

Out to the light, the surge of being alive jumped from body to body. Next up, lunch. The tricky one. The penny dinners. To blag in was a badge of honour. Meet the expert. Five gold medals.

Back down the quays. Quiet outside. People carrying cheap bags containing their lives. Big nun with headdress of high white wings controlling the door. I mean, really big. Frau Obergruppenführer. Our well-oiled plan springs into action. Four men up lane to hide.

I stand at back of queue, slightly out to side. Snivelling. Quiet sobbing muffled in dirty hankie.

Frau O comes down the queue. 'What's wrong with you?' she asks.

'Nothing,' I say.

'What's your name?'

'Kevin,' I say. No it isn't.

'Tell me what's wrong.' She leans down. She has a five o'clock shadow like Desperate Dan. 'Step over here,' she says. 'Whisper.' Stubble at mill.

'My da came home drunk and smashed up the house. He threw our dinner out into the street. He beat my ma with a chair. He put his fist through the telly and it's not even paid for. Me and my brothers ran for our lives. We slept under the canal bridge.'

'When did you last eat?' she asks.

'Thursday,' I say. 'We found a loaf under a Bewley's van.' I made that up on the spot. Raw talent. I'm wasted.

'Have you any money?'

'No,' I say, 'but I could give you my miraculous medal. One of my brothers has a penny. He could go in and bring a bit out for us.' All this blinded with tears.

'Get your brothers and follow me.' I like firmness in a woman.

In like Flynn. Sorted. Still bawling, huge hiccups. You can't fake a hiccup. Ask anyone.

Five of us at a long factory table. Then pure magic. Each knife and fork hanging on a little chain. Pilfer-proof. Brillo. I vowed that when I'm rich and famous I will have gold chains on my knives and forks. In a castle.

Queue. Four heavy steel bowls of steaming stew. Two lumps of bread. Margarine. Get it inti ya, Cynthia.

At the other end of our table, two tramps. Not a tooth between them. Arms around their stew and bread. Who's going to rob your stew when you 'can get it free up there'?

'Bugger off,' one tramp says. 'Cheeky pup.'

'What did you do with your teeth?' I ask him.

'I gave them to a Jap for a loaf of bread on the death railway in Burma.'

Was it sliced pan? I was going to say, but maybe in poor taste. I did not.

Sister Stubble panzered down the aisle. 'Have you stopped crying?' she asks.

'Have you any chips?' The Little Flower asks. She ignores him.

'All down on your knees for the Rosary,' she says, Desperate-Dan chin out.

'We will first go to the boys' room,' I say. A jiffy. Into toilet. One small window open. Polished team effort. Out the window and away like shit off a shovel. Rosary, my arse. There's no such thing as a free lunch. You'd want to be up all night, even the nuns pushing something. I ask you. Is nothing sacred?

Last item, 100-ton crane. Renew our plan to conquer it. At dock gate tell man our mothers sent us here to get money from our das before they went to the pub. In. Stand at legs of giant crane. Old, rusty, dignified, beautiful as an old lady can be. Gate closed with big chain and padlock, keep out. Bill Brown is the only man allowed to the top. You can see Wales from there. The magic was this: he told a hushed crowd one morning that he saw women playing tennis in Holyhead in little white frocks. Clear as day in the early morning light, in Wales. Wales. Never mind the U-boat during the war.

This would be our next outing. Bill drank with my father. Our plan, like all good plans, simple. Take his keys from overcoat when he was drunk in our house. Press into bar of soap like in the movies. Cut copy. Climb crane at dawn to wait for tennis and see women. Easy. One day.

Our work done, the Broadway Café. Bright lights, big city. I remembered my da had given me a note for when I got there. I opened it. It was a good note: a pound note. Geddit? Talk about excitement.

Call over waitress. The beautiful one. Tight red uniform, big smile, red lips. I fall in love as she walks over. Head over heels. My fifth time in love, I knew the score. Love hurts. She has a little white pad, a lovely little white pad.

'What's your favourite band?' I ask.

'None of your business, you cheeky pup.'

Opening gambit. There are many moves in life's chess game. 'Resistance is futile,' I say. 'Destiny calls.' Churchill, my hero, said that.

'Order or out,' she says. A fighter.

'Four sausage and chips with extra chips. Then four Knickerbocker Glories.'

'What colour jelly?' she asks, looking round the table.

Red. Red. Red. Green. There's always one.

Food comes. Like feeding the lions at the zoo. My uncle calls sausages 'widows' memories'. Quiet snigger. I go up to pay. Give her a sixpenny tip.

'Be patient,' she says, 'your time will come.'

'I was only showing off in front of my mates.'

'I know,' she says, and smiles and touches my hand. 'Wait. Just wait.'

As I said, love hurts.

Next morning debriefing at hideout. Snag did not show. Funny, that. Or the next day. Or the next.

Friday night sitting outside chipper. On our bench. Large singles. Mrs Fusco was famous for her one joke, delivered deadpan.

'Will the chips be long?' from the queue.

'About three inches.' Always funny.

Snag showed up and sat down. No hello. 'I'm out of the gang,' he said. I dropped my chips. 'I went to see the Spanish gypsy woman on my own.' Shocked silence. Chips on the ground cooling. 'I went twice,' he said. 'And we're going to the pictures.'

'Did you? ... Are you?' I stammered.

'Yes,' he said.

On that bench, on that night, at that hour, our boyhood ended, our gang broke up. Never saw him again. Word was he went to Spain with his lady. I hope he finds happiness. It's elusive. We all need to give it our best shot. Never did see the ladies in Wales. Pity.

9

SURE, A BIRD NEVER
FLEW ON ONE WING

'Bastard. Miserable, mean, selfish bastard,' a docker said to his mates as the excise officer passed by in his shiny Ford Anglia. Many heads nodded in agreement.

The car was his pride and joy. You know the type. Hand-cut, flowered house carpet on the inside floor and in the boot. Plastic flowers on dash. Extra wing mirrors. Special chrome hubcaps. He took the wife out on Sunday for a drive and parked at Dollymount strand reading the papers with the windows closed. Fresh air. They wore their slippers and cardigans, which they kept in the car for the purpose. Bastard.

A plot was hatched. Revenge is sweet. During a quiet lunch hour when he was up at head office a forklift expertly lifted the car and carried it to a container compound. Hundreds of eyes watched in cunning silence. It was lowered in front of an empty container with the doors open. Many willing hands pushed it through the doors, which were then slammed shut and locked. The container was bound for Bombay, stowed as deck cargo on a five-week winter passage across the Indian Ocean. The car vanished. Gone, never to be seen again. It was not tied down or secured in any way. The ship hit a typhoon. The slippers were the only thing not smashed into a small metal tangle.

The excise officer worked with his assistant, known as a producer, and a carpenter in a special high-security warehouse, which housed only expensive brandies, vintage wines, whiskeys, liqueurs. Their job was to tap sample kegs to check alcohol content for duty.

The carpenter used a heavy wooden mallet and chisel to open old casks. The producer inserted a long clear glass tube open at both ends. He dipped the tube into the cask and placed his thumb over one end. When he lifted out the tube it showed a sample. This was emptied into a glass phial by removing his thumb so that the liquid flowed. The excise officer then put the government-calibrated hydrometer onto the surface of the liquid where it floated at a depth dependent on the alcohol content. This was read off the side markings and entered into the log. The duty could then be assessed.

The sample was known as 'the angels' share' and traditionally the samples were shared out at the end of the day with a taste for all working on the ship. The officer changed all this. He put the samples into bottles and brought them home. Not a good idea.

There were also many gifts of expensive wines and spirits from grateful shippers and agents. Again, not shared. Again, not good.

Another plot was hatched. A strange piece of cargo arrived one day on a French shallow-sea vessel, an ancient brandy cask lying on its side and expertly roped onto a pallet. It was clearly marked as 'Nelson Trafalgar Brandy' and addressed to Professor Roland Lindon, Trinity College, Dublin. It was heavily sealed and embossed with red wax stamps. 'Sorbonne, Paris', it said. 'Do Not Disturb. Do Not Use'. An old docker removed this sign. Quiet laughing echoed around the nearly empty ship's hold.

The old cask swung out over the river as it came up out of the hatch and into daylight. It was carried by forklift into the excise store. There were many conflicting opinions among the dockers as to what it was. All experts to a man, of course. The received wisdom that this must be the finest and oldest brandy in the world, seeing as how it was being given to Trinity College by the Sorbonne, no less.

It lay in the cool dark warehouse for a few days while the excise man controlled his curiosity and worked out exactly what he would say in his report. He looked forward to sharing the angels' share with his friends rather than with coarse dockers who did not possess a palate subtle enough to appreciate such a renowned and rare vintage.

Next morning the three-man team set to work. The heavy red wax seal of the Sorbonne was gently removed, and the bung carefully opened. A rich, powerful aroma filled the air. Knowing glances were exchanged.

'Must be a hundred years old,' said the carpenter. 'The big shots and toffs in Trinity will enjoy this after their feast.'

The glass tube went in. The thumb was applied. The tube was extracted full of a dark, golden liquid. The thumb was removed and the precious fluid flowed into a glass phial. The cask was resealed with an Irish Customs Bond marker. Next day it was delivered to the professor in Trinity.

Word filtered back that the excise man and his wife and friends all agreed it was a life-enhancing experience to be allowed to taste this piece of history. The excise man's wife had a second small snifter. 'Sure, a bird never flew on one wing,' she said, laughing.

One week later two pieces of mail arrived at the excise office. A small parcel containing two pairs of slippers, one ladies', one gents', both badly torn by flying glass. Also a badge from a Ford Anglia. Attached to the letter was a photo of a small ball of metal sitting on Mumbai docks surrounded by a crowd of bystanders dressed in white robes for the intense heat. The letter said: *Sahib, it is with a broken heart and many griefs I send you metal of fine car much broken on the sea. With God's will the much unlucky owner will survive heavy sads and have many sons.*

The other was a letter from the medical faculty at Trinity College. Its tone was curt and ominous:

Sir, we are at a loss to understand why our recent shipment was interfered with. It was clearly marked 'not for consumption'. When Nelson was killed at Trafalgar, the defeated French gave a cask of finest brandy so that the body of the fallen warrior could be sent home tied to the mast of HMS *Victory to be buried in Westminster Abbey.*

To celebrate the historic joining together of our medical teaching faculties, the Sorbonne sent us a cask of brandy containing severed heads, legs, arms, fingers, eyes, ears and brains, all samples with diseases for study including cancer, syphilis, leprosy, plague and pox. All were in advanced stages of decomposition.

Should any of this material have fallen on clothes of workers or touched their hands, we advise an immediate and full medical examination. Please do not interfere with our goods in future. The Minister has been informed of our displeasure.

Signed: Professor Roland Lindon, Medical Faculty, Trinity College.

The excise officer did not have a good day.

10
GIVE US BARABBAS

Before containers, loose cargo came in cartons, packing cases, timber boxes, pallets, and often went 'slack', which meant broken.

Contents were visible and had to be stabilized so that at least the packaging was delivered for insurance count. It was signed off as STC ('said to contain') 100 dolls, say. You can imagine the rest.

The crews of ships also conducted a steady trade in goods that went in and out of fashion. Polish ships cornered the market one year in brightly checked lumberjack shirts. Large numbers of dockers, young and old, turned up for work looking like American folk singers, or student protesters. Another year, Chinese ships brought a flood of Chairman Mao blue padded work jackets, with toggles, as on a duffel coat. I wore one for years. They are now the height of fashion with trendy Southside social revolutionaries who have nothing and want to share it.

Barabbas drove a seven-ton forklift. He was a born hustler, or gifted capitalist entrepreneur, depending on how you see the world. His forklift had many gear storage areas, toolboxes, secret places. All of these where stuffed with a wide selection of goods to suit every taste. Bang on trend, bang on price. He conducted a thriving business as he drove around the docks visiting his loyal client base. They came to him for wedding and anniversary gifts and Holy Communion presents.

If he hadn't got in stock the item a customer wanted, he would take an order for it. That meant a gentle nudge of the rear of his forklift to the corner of a packing case as he passed by on his duties. 'Slack': are you still with me? Having made the necessary adjustment to the packaging, he didn't even bother to get off the forklift, but drove on. His hands never left his wrists, oh no, our boy was too wide for that.

During a pilferage clampdown, Barabbas was called to head office. Serious. He told the manager he was shocked and disappointed to be told that pilferage was happening in his workplace. He was ever vigilant and would immediately write a report if any incident happened while he was working a ship. He would name names. Show no mercy, as was only right and proper.

He was asked if he had ever pilfered. He said that last year he had eaten a bar when he was helping to tape up a broken pallet of chocolate. Fruit and nut. It had been on his conscience ever since. He had lit a candle to St Anthony, the patron saint of those who had fallen into sin. The manager sat in stony silence, and wrote down Barabbas's confession.

When word got out that Barabbas had been brought to the office, hundreds of dockers in between decks of several deep-sea ships started a chant:

'Give us Barabbas!'

'Give us Barabbas!'

'Give us Barabbas!'

It was meant to be funny but the voices of hundreds of unseen men coming up from open hatches to join their voices to the chant made for a strange and haunting scene, one that men would never forget.

Barabbas became a star turn in local pubs, being called on over and over to tell his story of the bar of chocolate and the candle to St Anthony.

On the last Friday before Christmas, after work at 5 pm sharp, he arranged his annual fashion and accessory show for his clients in the pub beside the Point Depot. This was the social highlight of the year – standing room only. Foreign seamen were welcome.

A small, bald docker named Jem became Jemima for the evening, and sashayed up and down before the crowd, modelling a selection of ladies' frocks, coats, handbags. 'Slack'. He got tumultuous applause, wolf whistles, offers of marriage, lewd suggestions; he was even pinched on the bottom. Barabbas gave a running commentary of fashion trends re colour, sleeve length, hem height, mix and match. He also set out in some detail the various outcomes when a grateful wife or girlfriend got her new frock, coat or handbag. Jemima, ever demure and in a ladylike fashion supported these few words with a small, tasteful mime, which left no doubt as to a positive conclusion. The packed pub roared their approval.

All items were sold 'off the model' as the show progressed. Jemima dressed and undressed for the client on the spot. Trade was cash only, no haggling allowed. Barabbas put all proceeds behind the bar for free drink for all. Sailors brought Polish vodka, Chinese brandy, blue and red liqueurs with names in strange script.

Each year there was a special surprise treat. One time, everyone in the audience got a huge bar of Toblerone, another year, expensive sunglasses. Jemima got her handbag filled from a grateful and adoring audience. The evening usually ended with arm-wrestling and the singing of cowboy songs.

In the new year Jem was promoted to 'singer out'. This meant standing on a platform on deck looking down into the open hatch and guiding the crane driver who could not see down into the bottom of the ship. The singers out used a rolled-up newspaper for better visibility. It was an important skill and brought safety to those working below, 'under the hook'. It was a little bit of theatre: the singers out were stars.

One day the wind swung a heavy hoist of timber the wrong way. It knocked Jem off balance, and he fell through the safety rail and down through all the decks to the bottom of the ship.

All work was stopped that day. His broken body, resting on a blood-soaked sheet, was lifted out on a pallet by crane for all to see. Men wept. Jem had been much loved. His huge funeral stopped all traffic, and went on for days.

The Barabbas fashion show never took place again. The magic was gone. When Barabbas saw his first container, he resigned. He opened a chain of shops and became a millionaire.

His fashion business offerings are now a must-have for the glitterati at the top of society. His brand name is 'Jemima', as it should be. Little do his customers know. 'The past is another country,' as the man said.

11
RATTLE

Vantastic. No. *Van Ordinaire.* No. *One Boy One Van.* No. *Boy Meets Van.* No.

I was going into the removals business. I needed a catchy name. I believe in starting at the top. School finished, beginning of summer. I needed work, I needed money. Serious money.

At seventeen, a motorbike, three girlfriends, drink, fags, party every night – it mounts up. My financial standing would not suit Mr Micawber. My father said I could use one of his small vans to look for work at the weekend. Perfect. Cut out interviews. Suited me grand, as I am crippled with shyness and crushed self-esteem. I am not a natural employee. I see myself as management.

In those days, antique dealers put their furniture outside their shops on Saturday mornings. Georgian furniture was cheap, there was no shortage. Big houses were selling up all over Ireland.

I printed my first flyer: *Across the street, around the world.* Modest, understated, my style. It set a tone, I

76

thought. Another one: *We will do anything for a fiver.* Not classy, too needy, a bit clingy. And: *Let us handle your drawers* (snigger). No, of course we did not use that one. Well, OK, a few times in the Bailey, my new office. Mixed results.

Saturday morning, sunny. An old Georgian Dublin street. Shops open, gear outside, lined up. People, mostly women, middle-class women, viewing. My assistant, not the sharpest knife in the box, it's hard to get good staff, handed out our flyer (*Special Saturday Offer*).

Bingo. Within minutes, a knock on the window of the van.

'Young man, will you bring my new table to Ranelagh, please?'

'Of course, madam, glad for the bit of work.'

A bit of cringing and forelock-tugging is always an earner. Posh ladies like it.

Table into the back of the van in jig time. Clean white sheet over it. Upmarket, as were our clients. The clean-white-sheet scam became our trademark, after I had robbed every sheet in my mother's house. I got caught and had to buy dozens of them in Guiney's in Talbot Street. Overheads can kill a young business, you know.

Into the gaff.

'I'm a collector,' she said, la di da.

'Our house is Regency,' she said. 'Derek is a barrister,' she said, 'he likes nice things.' Poor Derek.

'Put it over there,' she said. 'What do you think?'

'It would be better under the window,' I said, 'and lose the ornaments. Declutter.'

We moved it.

'You're right,' she said. 'You're a clever young man. What did you say your name was?'

'Cedric,' I lied. There's a taxman behind every sofa. I trade in cash only; tax was what you put on your car. Maybe.

'Cedric what?' she said.

'Cedric McGinty,' I said. I liked the sound of that, I might use it again.

She paid me £5 and gave me a £1 tip.

'What do you think of our collection?' she asked.

'Love it: taste, sophistication, in keeping with your beautiful home,' I said.

She glowed. Guff central. Lying bastard.

'What a lovely thing to say, Cedric, you really are a clever boy, you will go far. I'll book you again see you next week. Can I have a card for a friend?' she asked.

I gave her one with a flourish. She gave me another tip, another pound. Note to self: bigger cards.

And so it began, business boomed, I was run off my feet. Middle-aged posh women everywhere. I had a queue.

'I booked you first, Cedric. My sister is waiting to show you her pieces, we'll book you for the rest of the day.'

Remember, I was a spoofer, a blagger's guide, thirty years before blagging was invented. But I learned fast.

An old dealer saw I was bringing buyers into his shop and in one hour gave me a crash course in Georgian furniture. 'When in doubt, say "Everything after the Regent lost its purity."' It means nothing but stops questions. Perfect. I used it for years.

In one month, one short month, I was rich. Loaded. I had a wedge, wonga, folding, spondulicks, Nelson Eddies, bees and honey, Johnny Cash.

I drank only cocktails with little red umbrellas, Indian takeaways for twenty people, free poppadoms for all. Boots for the footless childer, fur coats for the homeless. Spend, spend, spend.

Then I met the two famous old gay dealers from London, and my real education began. They greeted me on the street. They had diamond earnings, flares, bouffant hair. They came to Dublin to buy good Irish furniture. Antique-trade royalty. They nicknamed me 'Irish'.

They booked me for the day. They were going to a big house auction down the country. I said I would follow their taxi. They said no, they would come with me in the van. I sang for them most of the way and they recited dirty poems. We stopped twice for drinks. I watched them at work that day. A masterclass, no blagging here. Deep knowledge, sophisticated taste, authority, work the room, formidable skill. I soaked it up, steeped my feet.

As they got to know me they told me if I saw anything I liked I was to phone them and describe it to them in detail. They sent a cheque when I bought for them.

All the time I was learning, listening, asking, turning things upside down: why is that? when was that? who made that?

On one of their visits there was a big reception in the city. As always, I brought them everywhere in the van; they just liked it. They phoned me later to collect them. They were a bit drunk. They said a rich heiress had invited a large group back to her house for drinks. A big mansion, gardens lit up, servants at the door, a line of limos. This was fur coat and knickers territory.

I dropped them at the gate. They said, come in. I said, no, it was not my place, they were not my people, I was too young. They said, wait. They came back out, and said the lady had invited me in.

The huge house was dazzling, blazing with lights. Great wealth has its own light, its own seductive pull. Smiling servants.

'Champagne, sir?' asked a young girl of my own age, and then asked with her eyes, What are you doing here?

'I'm with them,' I said, pointing to the two gays. They were wearing matching lilac satin suits.

'Oh,' she said.

'No, no, no,' I said. 'I *work* for them.'

'Whatever,' she said. She left with her bubbles and false smile. You can't win them all.

A senior government minister asked over the noise and music if he could see the famous collection of miniature elephants. Big shots and VIPs everywhere, all asked the same. They all wanted to see them. The lady wavered, but said yes. She also was a little drunk.

She opened the base of a tall bookcase and took out a large square tray with a dark-blue velvet cushion with indents. It held about thirty tiny, jewel-like objects, which burned when the light caught them. This was a world-famous collection. Like all great beauty, it caused a silence to fall and gathered to itself all light.

The lady set out to tell us what each thing was. The best was last. A thirteenth-century Indian elephant, solid gold, four inches long, tiny filigree red pattern across its back. The *howdah* (saddle, to you and me) in diamonds, glittering diamonds, hundreds of them. A little *mahout* (driver) seated with lapis-lazuli-blue turban. Each elephant foot encrusted with precious stones. Those are pearls that were his eyes. The tusks were of ivory tipped with silver. It stood on a bejewelled crystal cushion with pearl tassels all around. People gasped when she held it up to the light. It was dedicated to the loved one of an Indian king. It spoke of a time when there was no limit to labour or measure of cost.

The tray was passed along the extended polished table. Pools of silence followed it. Drinks were served. Finger food. The hubbub started up again. Dancing, people crowding around the trays of food. A ragged sing-song started. Some minutes later the tray came back down along the table on the other side. When it got under the light one thing was missing. The main one. The lady of the house said it was too valuable and fragile for a joke.

'Put it back, please.' Nobody moved, nobody spoke. She said it again, then again, then again.

'Stop the music,' she said, 'turn on all the lights. Put the piece back, now.'

Servants froze, smiles gone. Deadly silence, no one moved.

'Put it back *now*, this is not funny,' she said. A drunk started singing on the sofa. She snarled at him to shut up. Silence again.

After half an hour all were asked to turn out their pockets. Senior barristers, politicians, leaders, no one refused. All done in stony silence.

'I will call the police if this does stop now,' the lady said. No sound, no movement. The police came, took a look at the VIP guests. 'This is a civil matter. We're not getting involved.' They left.

A couple of women were weeping on the sofa. The minister said he had to go as his driver was off shift. Quietly, he left. Two other couples also left. I was told to go and get the van, which I did. The dealers came out and we drove home in silence.

The elephant was never found.

I worked a few years for the two gays. They retired and sold the huge stock of their big Chelsea house, shop and stores. They sold every single thing they had ever owned, every single beautiful thing. Forty years of the best the world had to offer. It made millions. They kept nothing except a little Elizabethan child's silver rattle. It dated from the year when the plague was raging in London. Shakespeare closed his theatre and went touring in that same year.

They bought a big, simple stone Renaissance house in the square of a rough Italian fishing village. They stripped out everything, down to the plaster walls. It was bare and empty, no possessions. Painted in white, filled with light. In the local shop they bought a modest sofa, a table and four chairs and a couple of beds. They would never own anything again. They asked me and my wife to stay with them.

They often rang me. They had breakfast each morning in the square with the locals. They went to the market and bought fish every day as the boats unloaded. They never left the village; it was their home. They bought a tiny second-hand Bambino, which they used to collect their wine from the famous local vineyard, which they owned.

Years passed. I heard from them less, they were old now. One summer morning I got a small box in the post with a beautifully written note. It contained the Elizabethan child's rattle, which had survived, in its innocence and beauty, five hundred years of man's madness. The last thing they owned. They told me I was the son they would have wanted, had they been straight.

They died within weeks of each other. I went with my family to both funerals. They were buried in the small local churchyard. I asked that the rattle be buried with them. They gave the house to the village as a social centre. There was a small photo on the wall, I'm in it with them in the van. That day we were singing the Beatles.

12

TUG

The last two heavy steam tugs in Dublin were built the old way in an English shipyard. Traditional craftsmen's hands working in steel plate and hot rivets. They were indestructible. Curved and flowed with the line of a woman. Shapely. They sat in the water, confident in their strength and beauty. Rakish maybe, gallant certainly.

They were maintained with precision and love and pride and respect for their high Victorian values of lost Empire and Nelson's navy.

The curved and sloping wardroom, saloon and captain's quarters were dressed in polished inlaid mahogany panelling, which glowed in the half light of small green lamps set into the bulkheads. The main table was buffed to a deep shine each day, and all brasswork was turned to gold. Seating was old but well-loved green leather. The floor was oak planking, swept each day so that it shone with wax. The little world of a gentleman's yacht.

There was a main bridge and all-weather topside bridge. Each had a six-foot timber wheel centre stage with brass-capped spokes.

The helm, compass, binnacle, telegraph, all freshly painted and polished, stood to attention, awaiting orders. Along the back wall a bank of pigeonholes, each with brightly coloured signal flags folded to origami perfection with toggles squared away. Behind that the captain's cabin with a daybed. Hospital-nurse-perfect pillows with crisp white sheets and green wool blankets embroidered with ship's name in red. A small brass-bound desk with admiralty charts, binoculars, leather-bound ship's log, all softly lit. A heavy, soft green carpet gave the cabin an unexpected air of comfort. It was a place where men spoke quietly.

The ship's bell seldom spoke but was Brassoed each day and its rope with a monkey knot was blancoed. Question: how many ropes on a ship? Answer: one. The bell rope – all the rest are lines. Remember that, you may be asked.

The stokers worked stripped to the waist. The floor was steel chequered plate, which glowed to burnished pewter from many years of work. All overhead pipework was lagged and painted a blinding white. The sky above a blue hanky in a small grating up on deck. The stoker kicked a hatch and a half ton of coal dropped to the floor at the mouth of the furnace gate. A number nine shovel threw coal to the back of the firebox. Then the door was banged shut and the floor swept. On a stormy night shift, the soft warmth drew an audience of advisers to its wooden bench, wanted or not.

The galley held a long-polished stove. Black as your boots. Big coal fire under deep-grated ovens burnt day and night. Heavy-weather brass piping held rows of scrubbed pots and pans. Knives, racked and razored, marched along the wall. Plates stacked in open baskets. Everything gleamed. All to hand. Ready for action. Stripped down.

No plastic, no convenience-ware in that time. Each day a hot meal was served, bang on time. Table properly laid. Each man with a square, setting out knife, fork, spoon. Centre table a long loaf baked fresh each day, sliced and buttered. Once a week a currant cake. There was jam on Friday. All sat down together, hands washed, no smoking, no reading at table. All proper. After the meal, quiet time, seamen used to long voyages before the time of TV. Men at ease in their own company. Reading, darning, making and mending, hobbies, writing letters, silence for two hours. Dozing. Resting.

The main steam engine. Oh, that most beautiful engine. Gleaming in full traditional colours; green, red, grey. All pipework golden copper and brass. All lagging to white. When working, a noise like a sigh of pleasure. It was hypnotic to watch. You could not look away. You could not look away.

The main beams rocked and nodded. Up and down, up and down. Controlled, ordered, majestic, mighty, splendid power. Called to mind God. It was so quiet you could hear a man talking over it. Finger-clicking rhythm; a woman would sway. Men trailed their hands along it. It was a warm and pleasing to touch. It spoke to you. It was alive. It was loved.

Job on. Big Japanese freighter up coast loaded down to the Plimsoll line. Yokohama, Liverpool, Dublin. Bridge telegraph rang out to engine room. Orders from bridge. All calm, practised, steady. 'Let go for'ard, let go aft, half ahead.' Mooring line coiled. Move away from wall, out into main river.

The westerly wind carried the smoke from the stack downriver, east and ahead of both tugs, out into the blue bay. Our wake, a spill of diamonds across the river gate to the city.

They steamed slowly in convoy. The light that morning would break your heart.

Captain and mate on fly bridge. Full naval uniform, fresh white lids on caps. The captain went to sea at fourteen years of age. Worked on the last four-masted sailing cargo ships up from Australia with wool, when the China tea trade collapsed. He told me that under full sail, a 'cloud of sail' he called it, they could beat any modern freighter across the Indian Ocean. Living history. Went aloft in all weather. North Atlantic winter convoys in the war. Canada to Murmansk in the Arctic circle. U-boats all the way. Slept standing up for two years, torpedoes in the night. Sub-zero. Force Ten. Men who knew no comfort.

Out past lighthouses, port and starboard, old friends. To remember port wine is red. Ship coming up away down on horizon. Both tugs gently turning into a big, lazy three-mile circle to come up under her bow and stern.

Ship's speed to dead slow. Lead tug inches under overhanging bow. High overhead, brown faces appear. Lascar seamen. No words, signs only. The language of the sea. Four-inch manila hawser snakes down from bowsprit and is captured by crew on tug deck. Secured to towing bollard. Looking aft, the captain makes international sign: both arms raised above his head, crossed at the wrists with both fists clenched. 'Made fast, secure, made fast.'

Ship is under tow. New rules now. Tug moves ahead slightly, line takes strain, a dangerous time. Tug settles down into water as weight comes down the line. The heavy wash scourges a deep-purple bruise on the face of the sea.

'All ahead slow' rings out on the bridge telegraph across the sweet, gentle morning air.

The throaty growl of a deep steam whistle booms out across the bay. One blast. 'Stand clear all shipping' and then the silence of a weekday church. Small waves slap the towering knife of the ship's bow high above us.

Flags snap and shiver in the wind, ruffled. The little procession enters port and turns into the berth. Past the old hailing station that long ago had a speaking megaphone, which asked 'What ship are you?' A heaving line shoots out from the deck to the quay. The cowboy lasso uncoils and as it flies is caught by a hogger. Two men release the bitter end and secure to mooring bollard. Ship's winches call in the slack and the ship inches to the quay and softly kisses the shore. Home and dry, safe and sound. Long, mournful blast on whistle, signalling all clear. Tugs let go and turn to home berth. They always lie together. Side by side, a team. Brothers in arms.

Smell of lunch cooking sharpens the air. Stew today, a favourite. Coffee to the captain's quarters. All hands stow and tidy in the silence.